Persistence and Other Poems

David J. Murray

iUniverse, Inc.
Bloomington

Persistence and Other Poems

Copyright © 2010 by David J. Murray

All rights reserved. No part of this book may be used or reproduced by any means, graphic, electronic, or mechanical, including photocopying, recording, taping or by any information storage retrieval system without the written permission of the publisher except in the case of brief quotations embodied in critical articles and reviews.

The views expressed in this work are solely those of the author and do not necessarily reflect the views of the publisher, and the publisher hereby disclaims any responsibility for them.

iUniverse books may be ordered through booksellers or by contacting:

iUniverse
1663 Liberty Drive
Bloomington, IN 47403
www.iuniverse.com
1-800-Authors (1-800-288-4677)

Because of the dynamic nature of the Internet, any Web addresses or links contained in this book may have changed since publication and may no longer be valid.

ISBN: 978-1-4502-7227-8 (sc)
ISBN: 978-1-4502-7229-2 (dj)
ISBN: 978-1-4502-7228-5 (ebk)

Printed in the United States of America

iUniverse rev. date: 11/20/2010

CONTENTS

INTRODUCTION.....................................IX

NIGHTMARES AND BACK-SCREAMS

PORTENT #1 2
PORTENT #2 3
NIGHTMARE #1 4
NIGHTMARE #2 5
NIGHTMARE #3 6
NIGHTMARE #4 7
NIGHTMARE #5 8
NIGHTMARE #6 9
NIGHTMARE #7 10
NIGHTMARE #8 11
NIGHTMARE #9 12
NIGHTMARE #10 13
NIGHTMARE #11 14
NIGHTMARE #12 15
NIGHTMARE #13 16
NIGHTMARE #14 17
NIGHTMARE #15 18
NIGHTMARE #16 19
NIGHTMARE #17 20
NIGHTMARE #18 21
NIGHTMARE #19 22
NIGHTMARE #20 23
EX-PARAMOUR......................................24
BACK-SCREAM #1 25
BACK-SCREAM #2 26
BACK-SCREAM #3 27
BACK-SCREAM #4 28
BACK-SCREAM #5 29

BACK-SCREAM #6 30
BACK-SCREAM #7 31
BACK-SCREAM #8 32
BACK-SCREAM #9 33
BACK-SCREAM #10 34
BACK-SCREAM #11 35
BACK-SCREAM #12 36
BACK-SCREAM #13 37
BACK-SCREAM #14 38
BACK-SCREAM #15 39
BACK-SCREAM #16 40
BACK-SCREAM #17 41
BACK-SCREAM #18 42
BACK-SCREAM #19 43
BACK-SCREAM #20 44
BACK-SCREAM #21 45
BACK-SCREAM #22 46
BACK-SCREAM #23 47
BACK-SCREAM #24 48
BACK-SCREAM #25 49
BACK-SCREAM #26 50
BACK-SCREAM #27 51
BACK-SCREAM #28 52
BACK-SCREAM #29 53
BACK-SCREAM #30 54
BACK-SCREAM #31 55
BACK-SCREAM #32 56
BACK-SCREAM #33 57
BACK-SCREAM #34 58
BACK-SCREAM #35 59
BACK-SCREAM #36 60
BACK-SCREAM #37 61

BACK-SCREAM #38 62
BACK-SCREAM #39 63
BACK-SCREAM #40 64
BACK-SCREAM #41 65
BACK-SCREAM #42 66
BACK-SCREAM #43 67
BACK-SCREAM #44 68
THE MORAL 69

PERSISTENCE

YOUR SPECTRE 72
SELECTIVE PERCEPTION 73
FUELS 74
THE WAY IT WAS #1 75
POST-MORTEM 76
SOMEWHERE ELSE 77
BLUENESS 78
UNBALANCED 79
EQUIVOCATION 80
A SPRING DELAYED 81
THE LYNX 82
THE TIMES WHEN I FEAR YOU MOST 83
VERITY 84
INNOCENCE #1 85
OVERTHROWN 86
INNOCENCE #2 87
THE BROWNS OF WINTER 88
THE FORESTS OF MY THOUGHTS 89
QUESTIONS, QUESTIONS, QUESTIONS 90
CONTROL MODE 91
MODERATION 92
WISHFUL THINKING 93

WHERE'ER YOU WALK	94
INFORMATION	95
NO ANSWER	96
LISTENING	97
EARLY TO RISE	98
ART AND ANTIPATHY	99
WHEN EAGLES MEET	100
ARROWS	101
CHANGE	102
SUNRISE	103
INEVITABILITY #1	104
INEVITABILITY #2	105
ENOUGH?	106
YOUR REVENGE? MY REPLY	107
DAMN!	108
BRIEF ENCOUNTER	109

INTRODUCTION

In this fifth volume of a series, in which I am putting into print poems I have been writing over some fifty years, all the poems have to do with remorse, regret, and rejection in the field of heterosexual romance. While scattered poems on these topics can be found in each of the earlier volumes, the exercise of putting 106 previously unpublished poems into the present volume has been both upsetting and uplifting. Because the initial perusal of them after many years forced me to go back to times of my youth, I found it upsetting to have to revisit those early years with their memories of discontent. On the other hand, it was also uplifting to realize that I had been able to overcome those discontents in part by writing the poems you will read here. The usefulness of poetry as a medium for relieving mental distress, by way of self-therapeutic outpourings, is now being acknowledged in professional care-giving and occupational therapy circles; I recently contributed to a volume entitled *Celebrating Poets Over Seventy*, edited in 2010 by Marianne Forsyth Vespry and Ellen B. Ryan, who are associated with both the McMaster Centre for Gerontological Studies and with the Tower Poetry Society of McMaster University in Hamilton, Ontario.

The poems in the present volume all describe unhappy romances that took place in the 1960s. The poems have at least two lessons to offer to readers of any gender or age. The first lesson is that memories of exceptional misery, in particular romantic episodes, will not fade away as time passes; they merely lie dormant and can be awoken readily if an incident in everyday life serves to remind you of that misery. For example, one might say hello to a stranger one has met on a bus—and unexpectedly find oneself recalling an event that had taken place on a bus years ago, when one was in the company of a person about whom the romantic memories are, to say the least, ambiguous because they vacillate between despair and elation.

The second lesson is that any strong emotion, but most notoriously that of frustrated romantic desire, can set one's brain-works jangling, so to speak, to such an extent that the first line of a poem can come, spontaneously and unexpectedly, to mind. Because events of the next few years can easily cause that line to be forgotten, it should be written down immediately, if possible, and then worked into a full poem at a later opportunity. I first became aware of this in my early twenties, probably in late 1959, when I was courting somebody I had recently met. It was a sunny day, and I had found myself walking in the direction of the building in which she resided. When I got there, I rested on the grounds of the building and found a short four-line poem coming almost fully formed into my mind. In the 'back-scream' set of the first collection of poems in this volume, a number of short four-line verses appear, each a complete poem in itself; their common progenitor was the discovery, totally unanticipated by me, that a heightened emotional tension can be expressed by the involuntary construction of a versified sublimation of that emotional tension.

The second collection in this volume, containing thirty-eight poems, is entitled *Persistence* because, as outlined sketchily in the first poem of the collection, all the poems were written *after* the end of a relationship that had actually included so many happy experiences that I have dignified my memories of my partner, appreciatively and respectfully, with the accolade of making her a royal among the women with whom I have been romantically involved. Partly through indecision on my part, the relationship ended, but ever since we parted, I have been pestered internally by "what if we hadn't broken up?" questions.

The first collection consists mainly of a set of forty-four back-screams, all of which were written *during* the early courtship I mentioned above. The relationship went awry partly because I lacked experience and partly because the person with whom I wanted to be involved behaved in a disproportionately ungiving manner, but there was no question as to the intensity of my initial desire for her, or as to the veracity of the slow poisoning of the poetry I was writing as it progressed from an overyouthful optimism to an increasing level of suppressed verbal hostility. I should note that I never informed the person I was courting about the existence of these poems.

In the formative stages of that relationship, I frequently had bouts of extreme anxiety as to how much unhappiness I might have to experience before there was a resolution, if any, of my endeavour. The twenty nightmares represent a recent recasting of those premonitions; they build up to the back-screams, whose origin is briefly told in the transition poem entitled "Ex-paramour." The whole collection, entitled *Nightmares and Back-Screams*, starts off with two poems of portent and is rounded off with a poem called "The Moral."

I am, again, most grateful to everyone who has assisted me in the preparation of the manuscript for publication, especially Sylvia Hains, Marissa Barnes, and Rachel Breau; my deceased wife, Esther, supported the publication of the first three volumes in this series. I also wish to express my gratitude and admiration to the editorial and design teams at iUniverse for their dedicated professionalism throughout the production of this book.

Nightmares And Backscreams

PORTENT #1

A blush of rose, parabola,
Is inflected in a rush of red
To soften the underlining
Of walls of blackened cloud
As if a building woke from a fire
And yawned and went to bed.

The rest of the sky is whitened blue,
Save yellow in the east, whereon
Are puffs and line-shreds scored
From the same enblackened cloud,
As if it woke from a heavenly dream
And found its clothes still on.

Nightmares are places our verses take us
And, with their bewildering *angst,* awake us.

PORTENT #2

You, my participant, you of my night-dreams,
Why do I see you, in this midnight moment,
When lights in my blackness sputter and dim
And I subside and sigh and see the death
Of all who hover and who hide from me,
The waiting warmth of what I lost? No scream
Is deep enough, no groan high-pitched enough,
To skate my shipwreck o'er my arid blackness,
As each sad episode blurs the trail
I'm failing to make in my bewildered homeland;
All that sings out is, I'm lost in grief for you—
My only dark portender of my truthfulness,
My bringer-on of darkest inner nightmares.

NIGHTMARE #1

Now is my blood all fraught with fear,
And even the things I hold most dear
Seem to be tinged with anxious awe;
Have I then broken an ancient law,

The law that says, "Thou shalt not kill,"
When *my* blood it is they mean to spill?
Only sheer death can clear me of this place
Where art becomes subservient to race.

I feel the surge of artworks on the seas,
Sighings of giants Aeoliac through the trees,
Watching triumphancies yielding to disease,
And aching iciness upon the breeze.

For you I can teach these icicles to melt;
Please let me kiss you, yes, below the belt.

NIGHTMARE #2

I see the waking world, its winking lights
In the soft grey dawn grow twinkling on and off,
While the Christmas colours tread like pit-a-pat
On stoops and porches isolated with snow;
The moon is massive but not wholly clear;
Marks leave their traces on its lunar white;
It stands in silence while the city wakes.
Machines get rid of rubble near apartments;
The streetlights spotlight the drifty snow stream
Of the drifting pavement, and a moving car
Spreads its white headlights in between the rows
Of houses spotlit in their Christmas dress,
Their last lights dozing, red and green and blue,
Waiting to waken when I hear from you.

NIGHTMARE #3

Aye, it is freezing, drifting; on the lake
Streamers of blue on green foretell the ice
That will grip the waters, stilling them.
My landscape stops to freeze; I am forced back

To see my lifetime replicatable.
Where, oh where, is an Esther made for me
Again, remodeled on a muse's master lathe,
Firm in her understanding of my mind?

Now comes my math again, stagnant whore
Who steals the tiniest vestiges of desire
And tames them into demonstration—proof
Of matter over mind, of temper'd lust;

To have no newness, just a repetition,
Is the last thing I could tolerate or want.

NIGHTMARE #4

I fear the final freeze-up of my dreams;
Drab are the colours that adorn the dawn,
And the shining moon that shines above the town
Sends not a shred of light to warm my schemes.

Milk I must buy, and garbage bags, go out
Into a coldness utterly unknown
To Greeks and Romans who festooned their homes
With garlands of sculpted marble, and devout

Plinths to adored ideals, and pedestals
To ideologies that sponsored rites
Celebrating the gods, whose endless fights
With goddesses spurted harmonies from their walls.

Thus dream I, sadly, of their purity,
But only because I grieve my lost security.

NIGHTMARE #5

I tread the inched armour of my ground,
Trembling for fear I tread on pain;
What happened in the past is still around,
And distant pain returns to haunt again.

I wanted thee: the undivided thought
Of thy calf and the lovely curve of thigh
And waist and hip send me distraught
And find in so-called love no alibi.

And *because* I want thee, I might lose
To somebody less sombre, less severe;
Somebody else might hold thee; he will choose
Whether to kiss thee there, or here, or here.

And my poor mouth, empty of any flesh,
Must tongue these unwieldy words into this mesh.

NIGHTMARE #6

No silence strikes so low as does a phone
That does not ring with your sane and cheerful voice;
So I pursue chimeras in my brain
At how, at paining me, you might rejoice!

I was too honest, straight, and square and boring;
Cursory tricks and stratagems of the mind
I do not have; I want a re-restoring
Of Esther, my straight, foursquare, and oh! so kind

Dead lover; there's no one out there strong and straight
And honest, contemptuous of wine and drink,
Dreaming of night although it's not yet late,
Dreaming of day as slowly the starlights sink.

I cannot fight my sheer terrestrial drive
To find a body who'll keep my heart alive.

NIGHTMARE #7

And on they trample, dreadful hounds—
Coursing, slavering over the fields, canines
Bared at the glowing sunshine that impounds
The end of daylight, and incarnadines

The glowing blue of the late forfeited day,
And scatters scarlet across the banking clouds
While the hounds bay, clamouring for prey,
Veering themselves into knots and packs and crowds.

What are these dogs, these angry profligates
Who waste their loudness on the setting sun?
They are my verses, sorry delegates
Of my moods and longings, quite undone

By their intensity and ready to pound each page
With teeth and anger, bloodiness, power, and rage.

NIGHTMARE #8

Glowing with health, the fierce Auroric sun
Stood in a statued pose, casting his arrows
Of heat to the heavenless earth-built ground,
Counting as victors those whose flame sparked seeds
To grow, and disclaiming the squibbish ones
Whose flares entered water and were quenched.

Without a movement, without an elbow bent
Or a shoulder flexed, flexed the sun a bow
Of rare Platonic metal forged, and fired
Down to the same earth-treasured hell-less ground,
Counting as victors those whose flame sparked flowers
To burgeon from the seeds, and neglecting openly
The targeted arrows that were lost in water.

A statue filled with movement that stands still
Is well designed, a poet's heart to kill.

NIGHTMARE #9

I stand, scarped and really unholy, a fledgling
Combination of Leda and Narcissus,
Here on a hill by the edge of a city,
While my monstrousness spikes my brow with fear,
And endless perambulators of the young,
Filled with young babies with eyes of brown or blue,
Are pushed around beneath me—continuity.

Poseur I am not, for nothing posed
In concrete or mahogany can cause
Skittery words to flail the harbour ice
To manufacture sentences of prose
That seem the spewing of a self-taught child
Staring his way through a forest land of future
Where only what he stirs with words is real.

NIGHTMARE #10

Escape is the word that freely soars aloft
On crested wings with honeycomb designs,
While the burning bird of my soul lies languishing
On the ground that was sown and flowered by archers' arrows,
And tries to unearth a union with thee.

Oh, thy treacherous skirt falls, full and manifest
With discovered and new desire, falling to hide
Legs that remind me of whitened recollections;
It falls to keep itself from me, should I act
On my desire to bind myself to thee and it imprudently

By donning your skirt and thereby rediscovering
How you and I started with our stark betrayal
Of natural urges to play with one another;
Thus gilded we the silence of a sunrise.

NIGHTMARE #11

Those who answer questions suffer more
Than those who ask them; those who ask the questions
Suffer less than those who answer them;
And aphorisms squat like stones among proverbials.

NIGHTMARE #12

I write this fresh from a giant conjoint encounter
With thee in a thought-space wholly filled with thee,
By thee, over thee, under thee, and, yea, within;
Oh, thou art sculptress of my miseried world
Where a poem's worth less than a well-picked dirty word,
And a sonnet consists of two and a third sextets.

No words can match my fantasies of thee;
In a perfection so perfected with perfection
That imperfections are sores that scamper off
The moment infinity rears its perfect head,
I place thee where remembrances eternal
Fuel future fantasies with future thee.

Thee I adore, but fear thy *Schadenfreude*;
In thee I bewail thy glints of cruelty.

NIGHTMARE #13

When my hand stops, and stiff is my wrist from writing,
Nevertheless my thoughts go on of Eros,
And my hand goes down, tempted to sometimes stop
And touch me at the source of all perfection.
But writing preoccupies brain-parts unerotic,
So nothing happens while I seek new lines;

But if I rest from writing and survey the curtains
Red that array my windows and that hide
From me the outside hills and streets and houses,
Derelict now in a brown of stiffened snow
And scattered with leafless blackness of branches,
The curtains' red reminds me of a blanket,

Red, that I use as a covering for the bed
Wherein I've known thee only in my head.

NIGHTMARE #14

Poet, do not rest, unless it be from fear
That madnesses from tragedies of the past
Draw up their wings and start to hover near
Your pristine blue to make it overcast,

And ready to render hopes of tender longings
To spatters and splinters on a workman's floor,
And ready to tease, with twiglets of belongings,
Horrible tunes from memories of before,

And ready to grasp, with angelic-seeming smilings,
All that you hoped had gone, and stir it anew
To a broth bereft of any reconcilings,
A brew of sheer stress across the pristine blue;

No, do not rest, unless it be from fear
That those are angel wings you think you hear.

NIGHTMARE #15

Long have you hovered, my angel with demons for eyes,
On the edges of my long horizon's slopes;
All that is good shines out from your enterprise
Of understanding how hopers share their hopes.

But badness is treachery, waiting to filter out
Like an optic illusion whenever you laugh and drink
And drift, as if you never had a doubt,
Into the arms of whom I dare not think.

And all that's moderate lies there like a lion,
Firm in its marvelous mane, sleeping all day
But rising to yawn and parade dominion,
Searching for innocents on whom to prey.

All that you were seemed angelic; your skirt was white;
But now what your skirt hides haunts me every night.

NIGHTMARE #16

You have played upon my anger,
So I cannot see you more;
That glint, as you laughed at my abstinence,
Showed malice I only deplore.

I did wallow, once, in the peace
That alcohol brings to us all,
But I dare not indulge now, and therefore
I dare not even recall

How I loved laughing and flirting,
Sought lips that took tension away;
Then my mind moves to you; will *you* wallow,
Happy, for once, to display

How happily normal you'd be
If freed from the spectre of me?

NIGHTMARE #17

Oh God, what pain methought it was to mourn
The passing of your shoulders from my room,
The incontinent verbiage of your brilliant thoughts,
The embloomed rapture of your catlike feet
On my desk as you fixed a block against the sun
So that the screen could be seen unblemished,
Unmanacled from the mirrored lights that shone
Like irritating tanks ready to open fire
At anyone who hoped to read the writing.
I dare not love thee now; you've cast a pain
That only reminds me that I must lose again
Vernacular perfection of pure form,
The beauty of hair adown a lovely neck,
While I write this evil just to hurt you back.

NIGHTMARE #18

When I was young, a hapless twenty-three,
I could not think of anyone but she
Whose verdant flavours, poise of chest and arm,
Filled me with want, never to do her harm,

But just to join in with her in timeless play
Of two or three times every single day.
But our talk grew empty, sceneries grew impure,
And I my actor-self could not endure

Because reality was, I only knew *my* touch,
And showered my bounties like a daily crutch.
I dreamed of her, yes, naked in my grip,
Litheful and wondrous, ecstatic from her hip

To her golden groin above her golden knee;
But reality was, those "hers" were "mine" or "me."

NIGHTMARE #19

Although berserk with melancholy ways
Of feeling that my nightmare held a truth,
I cast them all aside to tell to thee
That you have learned that little that is good
Springs from that momentary fearlessness
That lets a taunt emerge, not understood,
Not met before, from your most inner thoughts.

By accident, I recently hurt my cat
When I closed the refrigerator door and caught
His head in that doorway's over-narrow gap.
He leapt out backwards, while I, quite horrified,
Pulled the door open again. The sense of disgrace
That shook me after my carelessness felt, for me,
Like something you felt after thy *gaucherie*.

NIGHTMARE #20

If I palpate an innocented look,
Scare-deer or hare, upon your beauty's face,
Nothing but pleasure should be the thing you took,
And honour should I receive, and simple grace.

But really, you rarely deign to show
What you truly believe behind that great display;
You move your lips nearer but desire for me to go;
You present your cheek, but you hope I'll go away.

Oh my innocent child, with very few demands,
How well concealed beneath your gentle smile
Is your bequeathèd hatred of those hands
Men want to touch you with, the while

They feel erection take the greater stage
To prod them into pushing, hold, and vice,
While you, in your heart's revulsion, rage
And freeze your feigned empathy to ice.

EX-PARAMOUR

Should I compare this incident to that
When someone I knew, but never really knew,
Raced into my life and so disgraced
My poet-life that tardy Time has placed
A jeopardy on my memories of what
Should never have happened, but actually came true?

In that appalling episode, I was young,
And she was selfish, spoiling a clever match;
Although I'd count the days before we'd meet,
Our every rendezvous was bittersweet,
Fettered within irrational moods that swung
From depth to depth with nauseous dispatch.

And nothing good came out of them except
A trail of poems marking where we'd been;
Back-screams I call them now; they're from the past,
So I feel free to bring them out at last;
But every line is a sign of where I'd wept,
And every sentence should have been obscene.

BACK-SCREAM #1

This tree is me and I a branch:
Its knocking heart my vessel is,
Its leaves are arteries for my blood,
And every bough embarks a flood
Of withered yellow memories.

Our lover's bond, no knife can staunch,
The slender sunny flow that flutes
A leafy filament around
Our souls in sapling veins enbound
And bids us breathe in lungèd roots.

And birds that hop and screech and call
Impinge their claws on *my* poor skin,
And shake *my* eardrums with their din,
My tree, this body, two, one, all!

BACK-SCREAM #2

I ride you, my tree, my thighs
About the lengthy ashness of your boughs;
Upon my paper leaps the leafy sun,
While stretch the fields beneath and insects run
And hailing birds sail white across the skies;
I ride you, my tree, and feel your blood-sap rouse.

BACK-SCREAM #3

I walked across the woodland meadow
Where in hail-beams hung the rain
Like atmospheric laurel-boughs
That spanned the fields and bore the brain
Up, up, to lands where rainbows fled
And lake-god ladies bore the pearls
And diamantine water drops
That from the crystal heavens bled;

Oh the inseparate dialogue
Of land and multifrice of light
Within a raindrop's shiny hand
From heaven taken flight!

BACK-SCREAM #4

Here as I lie
With my gaze in the sky
On a rambling cloud that embraces the breeze
And touches the ferniest tipples of trees
And kisses the plains
And caresses the rains
And fondles the mountains that hump through the air
Oh, sadly through branches, through branches, I stare
For to pull the sun down
And wear as my crown

BACK-SCREAM #5

Spring summer summer winter, she is there,
The laken depths of girlish eyes:
"Come," she cries, "I banish care"—
I come and winter summer summer spring,
Her raven hair blows on, come on,
And when I get there, she is gone,
Although the fields still hear her sing—
I try to love, and when the gate
Is banged against my face, I try to hate.

BACK-SCREAM #6

"Father night, where is your daughter?"
"In a sun-shell curled,
Where I left her,
Weighing the world."

BACK-SCREAM #7

Ganymede and peace are you,
My love, the falling and the aim;
No beauty breaks the bond between
You and the Peace that is your name;
And thunder gods shall break their bolts
And turn their heads away in shame.

BACK-SCREAM #8

You are the one who sets my pen on fire:
Small, bouncing, a bright eye and a clear wit,
And scrappy little hairs springing out of your head,
And dirty little feet you can't get shoes to fit.

BACK-SCREAM #9

Here flings sea-spume
Mountains high;
Over the horses leaping, bales light
Deep swales, liquid
Between wave-heights splashing;
Here scale Nereïdae
Planches of sea and sun
And down to glass
Leap.

This sea,
Italian structured,
Bathed though in *extases*,
Neither wind nor cold has
To chain to tresses,
Frozen as fountains,
Nereïdae hair.

Where?
Take wings
Or ride
Or in sense,
No sea without wind
Or cold
Exists;
Yet here
Are Nereïdae, who,
From the splinters of sea-blown
Spume, high and leaping
Emerge.

BACK-SCREAM #10

Gods who paint
Into Persephone the golds
And of dying day the greens
Drop, as mercy,
Onto the sleep-bound earth their peace;
And where squirrels
And stone martens love,
And stares the ibex,
Creeps the night and sleep;
And where, upon a ground
Breathing as of sleep, you lie,
Bring the gods peace
As a woven carpet to wrap you.

BACK-SCREAM #11

My girl, I want to take you and show you
The splendours of sunlight as they fall upon my eyes;
I want to divide your heart and bestow you
With half of the light that in my heart lies.

But, O sweet my girl, sometimes it's bare,
And then there's no light anywhere, anywhere.

My girl, I want to take your hand and go with you
To lands where brilliant flame the orange trees;
I want to laugh by the sand and blow with you
Clocks from the flowers of the Antipodes.

But, O sweet my girl, when my heart is bare,
There is no brilliance anywhere, anywhere.

And, O my girl, I want to enrapture you and fly you
To lands over the clouds where the gods blazen their halls;
I want to share with you god-laughter and hie you
To where laugh nymphs and leap deep waterfalls.

But, O sweet my girl, when my heart is bare,
I cannot take you anywhere, anywhere.

BACK-SCREAM #12

She could not a starling from a throstle tell,
But the wink of their feathers stood for her
As for a boy who foxes from wolves cannot tell
Save that both bark and are fierce and have fur.

She could not a daisy from a dandelion tell,
But she knew that both grew open flowers
As for a boy who oaks from cypresses cannot tell
Save that both give a climbing-happiness for hours.

BACK-SCREAM #13

To diapase your breasts with life
And clothe with skeins your silken form,
The night itself would wield a knife
To cut the daylight from the morn.

And when the dawn called mists and May
To clarify the light of men,
The night would steal a scimitar
From heaven's light to wield again.

BACK-SCREAM #14

We wandered over mire and dell
Until the stars turned in the sky
To golden boats and sunswept morn
Blazed a banner white and high.

We wandered till sunset drew her head
Down behind the dark green hills
And turned our backs against the sky
And lay down by the tumbling rills

And slept till morning drew her hair
White across the eastern sky
And sunwrapped clouds erased the night—
We slept because we wanted to die.

BACK-SCREAM #15

If, when the sunlight shoots between the leaves,
You catch the scarlet of a growing flower whose head
Strains to catch the sunlight and achieves
The lust of a boy catching a ball, be led
To treat it, by you, as a sign that the flower that strains
For sunlight will attain the light; but the flower
That hangs from the heat and droops from the summer rains
Is incompetent to deck the enchanted bower,
Or run cool hollyhocks' nectar from her stem
Encased in floral glory, because her heart
Is earthward turned, and though a hardened gem
Be pregnant, it must admit to be a part
Of a softer bubble, sick, without the gorged
Completion of a ruby sunlight forged.

BACK-SCREAM #16

I'm tempted to call you a flower,
But flowers die;
Still, it wouldn't be a bad thing,
For so shall I.

BACK-SCREAM #17

I think I love you, dear, because
I know that in, say, fifty years,
When you are fat and wrinkled, I
Shall still be on the verge of tears.

BACK-SCREAM #18

"I welcome old age with open arms
Because it brings me nearer death."
How shall I read this when happiness
Brightens my eye and burns my breath?

BACK-SCREAM #19

I'll fight dragons for you, scour
The earth, battle with ice and fire;
But don't ask me to be a hero,
For then I'd be a liar.

BACK-SCREAM #20

Once there sat, beside a sea
All wide and flat and cold,
An ancient god of eighty-three
Whose mind was young, whose face was old.

And by his side, beside the sea,
Breaking with splinters now of gold,
Sat there a youth of twenty-three
Whose face was young, whose mind was old.

BACK-SCREAM #21

Do not love the mists of men,
Only love the strength within;
Flee the ravages of fear
And analyze the sense of sin.

But curse, oh curse the kind of thought
That hides the feelings deep within;
For passion never marred the man
Who's analyzed the sense of sin.

BACK-SCREAM #22

Love is made on strength,
Cheerfulness and a call to respond,
Being ready,
But not to step beyond.

She did not find strength,
Cheerfulness or a call to respond;
He was not ready,
So they did not step beyond.

BACK-SCREAM #23

Sorrow, when it falls, has the freshness of a summer flood;
Leaves of glistened freshness hang their fingers in its flow.
Sorrow, when it rises, has the tingling of the blood
And climbs between the branches that were drooping down below.

BACK-SCREAM #24

Today as I was walking between the college walls,
I thought, "Now, am I really mad?" and answered "Am I balls!"

I wandered on between the bricks and soon came to the green
And thought, "But why then think I'm mad?" and answered "'Cos I've been."

And then I turned and saw thy face set in a woman's grin
And jerked my blurred eyes skywards and saw the clouds cave in.

BACK-SCREAM #25

My girl, I want you. Oh, I can lie,
Swearing my love is as pure as you earn,
But the sight of a tight little skirt in the court
Suffices for my lust to burn.

But listen, my girl, before you go:
If it wasn't thus, my love would die,
And admiration, cold as my brain,
Would ruin our love eternally.

BACK-SCREAM #26

I cannot whisper lovers' secrets
For they are always empty cheer;
Only the hopes and fears of one
Merit the other's hope and fear;
And hopes and fears of one must be
Concealed by love's diplomacy.

BACK-SCREAM #27

We gazed up with single eye
At the night black and free
And the moon a scimitar.

We counted stars in the blue-black sky,
Waiting to see who first would be
To see the morning star.

When climbed a cloud from low to high
And hid the stars, and we
Seemed from morning far.

BACK-SCREAM #28

Who comes there, swinging over the hill?
Lover Man! His eyes set for the kill,
The helm of valour, a Tristan's desire,
An Aucassin's beauty, an Abelard's fire!

Who comes there, singing the strength of love?
Lover Man! His noble brow sits above
His laughing eyes, clean, strong, and sane—
My God, I'd like to smash his brain!

BACK-SCREAM #29

The long dangers of introspection fall apart
At the loving comment of a loving heart;
The breaking questions and swirling lies
Of headstrong imagining vaporize;
And glimpses of emptiness to be
Drown in the lamplight of sympathy.

BACK-SCREAM #30

"Loneliness nor persuades us of the truth of thoughts
Nor company the lies with which fantasy teams;
Only the mood of the moment gives us the truth:
That our thoughts are our moods reclothed in dreams."

I write this deeply; for, falling in love,
I took a voyage into my soul so deep I nearly went mad;
There I found that events had no bearings on thoughts or on dreams,
And that thinking of thoughts tore away all the dreams that I had.

BACK-SCREAM #31

My life's not young, my life's not old;
My life is neither green nor gold;
But all I pray, O God of May,
Is that my life be never cold!

My life *is* young, my life *is* old!
O God of May, oh make me bold,
Bold to scare the draughts away
Of Winter's breath and Winter's cold!

BACK-SCREAM #32

If grief once grips the cord
And drenching pain the heart,
There is no consolation in art,
But there is in love.

If love once grips the cord
And love entrains the heart,
Then life is love, and life and art
New lovers prove.

BACK-SCREAM #33

My girl, your mind is free and wild
And wanders wildly as a child
Would wander over field and glen
Seeking to hide its hate of men.

My girl, I beg you keep your mind!
Let it go on, hating mankind!
For then, perhaps, in sympathy,
It'll look down, merciful, on me!

BACK-SCREAM #34

Blue of carnation revolves to rose
As were colours the reflection
Of waiting and passion
As shot they down the pass
Of memory's glass
As flowers fall, dying, to earth
To give rebirth

BACK-SCREAM #35

Images have I in plenty,
But each is a spear
Boring itself into my head.

Each is a spear
Fashioned from in-between times,
Between the kiss and the first embrace.

I have no images for night,
For that is sufficient to itself,
Dark and all-embracing.

BACK-SCREAM #36

Lost in a deep cold pride, he stood
Casting memories on the land like bones
Of animals scorched to death by sun
And watching them roll still among the stones.

Lost in a deep dark pain he seemed
Like a scarlet flower dragged to night
And darkened by a grief of never seeing
The gold of day or the white of light.

Lost, lost, and gone forever
Into a land that only he could tread
And potter among the bones of his years
Until his loneliness ate him dead.

BACK-SCREAM #37

When trumpets reiterate the violence of
"It is done and unredeemable! Die!"
I draw my breath and clench my fist
And snarl my challenge at the sky:

"No! I can fight! I can be another!
Only the one that acted need succumb!"
But if my voice is drowned and blocked,
I feel the tears begin to come.

BACK-SCREAM #38

My sweet, your hand and heart
Deprive me of all art
And kill my art-self dead,
For all my blood, instead
Of playing a creative part,
Goes rushing to my head.

BACK-SCREAM #39

"My darling, you must warm the hearth
And send the sparks to scare the night
I feel advancing 'round the world,
Bending its back to hide the light."

"My darling, why? The night is here,
The moon is here, the stars are here;
I have no terror of the night,
So let us love and no more fear."

BACK-SCREAM #40

I could not tear my mind from dreams
But breathed the dreams into all I saw,
Whispered the dreams into all I heard,
Weakened with dreams the simplest law.

I broke me from dreams, and all grew clear;
A woman's smile broke me away
From "women are goddesses," and I saw
How the world for me had gone astray.

BACK-SCREAM #41

Now we go into a deeper night,
And I, my love, shall play for you
The starlit jangles of our love
Upon a harp of heavenly dew.
And I shall hang, from treetop boughs,
The birds of our desires,
And, bright against the moon, we'll see
Their cages gleam like fires.

And I shall entwine for you, my love,
Long, deep blood-laces from their bars,
And hang from them the crystal tears
I plucked from overhead your stars,
The stars of pain I saw you stir
With your hand from the water-leaping sky,
And red into the firmament
Draw bright, as them to magnify.

And from the cataclysms of the pain-
And heaven-light that overflood
The present stars and trees around,
I'll weave for you, with love and blood,
A helmet, love, to shield you from
The dreadful fireflies' fearful light;
And on your helmet shall I sew
The stars and bird-song from our night.

BACK-SCREAM #42

Suns of crystal bend to fold
Arachne's web within their gold;
Moons of mica twist their beams
To spin the fireflies in their seams;
Stars of Sinai fire bend down
The burning beetles' wings to crown;
But what can night and day do
Fitly to array you?

Light can pull a cinder-wing
Down from skies o'er everything;
Rain can pull a brittle shower
To ease the heart and cool the flower;
Snow can turn a slow-worm flight
To shield the day-dew from the night;
But what can night and day do
Fitly to array you?

BACK-SCREAM #43

How can eternal passion live when passion pulls a face at love?
There could not grow upon a desert tree a finer flower
To hold the faintness of the sunset than that which brought
Us together for our fruitful hour
Solitary; but there grew and blushed, a phoenix unwanted,
The canker of a scarlet bloom which caught
Only the searing beams of noon
And scorched out love till the tree flaunted
Only a coral hardness to the moon.

No, it need not have been. Like a dodderer
Criticizing his books, I can desiccate
My actions. Like a critic speculating on effects,
I can analyze your motives. But I would rather hate
Than this blankness to mortify and freeze
As the slow sap of winter directs
The branches to congeal before the spring resuscitates
The glorious trees.

BACK-SCREAM #44

Like crosswinds on a fragile sail
Our hearts collided;
Named we the winds "hope of love"
Or "hope of loss of self," it matters not;
Neither of us won our lot,
And we remained divided.

Goethe wrote of elements
Affinitive in desire;
We were those called mercury
And iron, and these don't melt
Easily to each other; so each felt
Only the kindle of the fire.

THE MORAL

Round and round the seasons go,
From summer rains to winter snow;
And on and on the longings thrive
To copulate and stay alive;
And down and down the sunsets set,
Poems and compliments to beget;
And up and up sunrises rise,
To hail whomever's glorious eyes
Gaze into mine as I get old,
And poems get wrote, and tales get told.

PERSISTENCE

YOUR SPECTRE

As if you were a Royal Queen,
Your spectre still holds sway;
Bright are the lights from yesteryear,
Darkening what's today.
But dark are those images as well;
None are for mere display;
So out they will, and out they must—
You haven't gone away.
Swirling like larks upon a hill,
They swirl as if to say
That every word you see confirms
That in my mind you stay;
And were you here, I might address
You as "Your Persistingness."

SELECTIVE PERCEPTION

Is this not strength that, into the blueness of your eyes,
Caught in a filter of sentences I happen to say,
I can infuse desire yet still stop still in surprise
At the blueness they pour, into mine, of reciprocate skies?

Then why do I fear when, in a tip of your finger,
I can find more than ever I found in your eyes,
And "Stand!' "Stop!" "Still!" and "Move!" are sounds that linger
Before the engulfments that also drown the singer?

FUELS

Short though these lyrics are, they are formed
From the bending of rainbows
Round the limbed bole of a tree.

And forced though some seem, they are carved
From the splashing of waterfalls
Round nymphed rocks in the Antipodes.

And burned though some are with emotion,
They are fueled with flames
Fired when Athena engendered my battle-war.

THE WAY IT WAS #1

The day begins; there is cold and sacred blueness
That the pale cover of ongoing rain clouds
Can hardly haze; the bloom of jasmine
Has purple undiscovered by the sun, and in the roar
Of the growing city, hangs only incipience.

And there, as the day begins, still you sleep;
I know you are sleeping, for silence
Is holding its terrible pall over where you sleep,
And the sun has not yet enlivened
The silken threads of your head,
Nor has it uncovered
The loveliness of the arms you will bare to the sun.

And there, as the day begins,
I, sleepless,
Stand, wonder, walk, wait,
And cast, in a framework of delicate shadows,
These words over your still-sleep-enshrouded enchantment.

POST-MORTEM

I brought you through to a place of fierce fire
Where the wailings of dragons burned terrible holes,
To be pieced together with wings of desire;

And the wingings of thought are caught on the wings
Of an eagle suspended on high wings of air;
From every hyperbole, ecstasy sings.

When asked for, love becomes a game
Of hopes and, hopefully, hollowed fears;
Unasked for, love is not rightly its name.

SOMEWHERE ELSE

My cornered eyes are drooping with dull sleep;
Announcements augur, from my brain's recesses,
That I *must* sleep; and yet my pen flows faster
Than my blood, blots out images, and novel sense
Reticulates from meanings and conjunctions.

I feel my body lax and frisk the sheets;
Where is she? Where is her hair? Where is her head?
Where are her arms? Where are her warm emoluments?
Not here; she is elsewhere; elsewhere she sleeps,
And her eyes are lullabied by another's touch.

My head grows lax; my pen grows hard to hold;
The light's too bright, my intellect is dull;
I feel the wash of slumber mud my mind.
She is not here; her hair spreads somewhere else.
My eyes grow dull; they have no shine or lustre.

BLUENESS

The faltering haze of June bequeaths
To your eyes the trembling
Of the teeming rain that folds,
Into its hazy nectar,
The blueness of folded night.

To liken them to sapphires among stones
Would encourage hardness;
Their softness is of flowers
Or melted jewels, yet firm
They are like irises.

And when they glint with liquid, tears, or hurt,
Or anger or desire,
Their light is hammered lightly
Into sensuous responding
To an applicant air.

UNBALANCED

I bore the secret lashings of her eyes,
And the black whip of her intention
Furnished songs that spooked the skies;

And through the glooming cloud-gloom, where
The incessant fire of her laden pupils
Bore their elicitations, air

Flooded my countenance with sullen mien
So black it seemed to banish her
And drive me back into my den,

Once more a captive of my hidden fears;
And the warm waves of sweetspring seas
Bordered my solitude like tears.

EQUIVOCATION

Borne upon waves of crested flood and light,
I stand alone and stare
At the way I seem to have two selves:
I exult and I despair.

For exultation comes from power,
From the deep sea-surge's might;
And despair comes from reality
Where nightmares war with night.

So *must* I be a statue
Of Notness veiled in cold?
No, if I can't forget her;
Yes, if I plan on growing old.

A SPRING DELAYED

So sinks into the evening mire
The bewildered dust of daylight;
Nighttime hangs a dullened lamp
To illuminate the wayside.
Small fogs of evening hang,
Rampant, mute, and indolent,
Over the land's indentings,
Pockets, moles, and sullen bays.

Such a night were not the sort
To enliven verses, or inspire
A novel Cressida melody;
Yet it can be caught in a picture
Which, though grey, still represents
A physic fine and bolder.
The peace that some men have
In a passive starting spring
With no flowers or leaves, no high
Glad clouds, no whistling birds,
Just grey, is a poet's regimen.

THE LYNX

Padded and foot-sure,
He prowls through the forest;
Pine needles develop beneath
Each silent footfall;
He is a cat, large
And foot-sure; his food
Will be a torn
And battered bird.

THE TIMES WHEN I FEAR YOU MOST

The times when I fear you most
Are the times when I am clear,
Happy like a playing child,
Because I know I am loved.
And suddenly, a flicker of a page
Shows me cities we both visited,
And I am devastated.
My poor black brain searches
And gropes to close the door
So that nobody can see me,
And my face is an oldster's,
Torn by a winter
That knows no relief
From the wind that turns itself
To ice surrounding fire.

VERITY

Poets, they say,
Should praise the living love-look of her eyes,
Raise interplenary praise from her hair,
Admire in sculptured words her hoarded form;

But I
Will praise instead her darkened passageway,
The immensity of its flow, the dark corridor
That holds me fast, the bordered corners

Of open
Living flesh, inside of her but outside, open
To the entrance of shuddering me, and giving strength
To the unembellished movements of my will.

INNOCENCE #1

When nonchalance and innocence
Play games upon a tree,
Each leaf is full of sunlight;
Its sunlight falls on me.

When hate and fear and passion
Play games upon my brain,
Each tree that could be shivers
And shrivels into grain.

OVERTHROWN

Must I, when I think of you, be so overthrown
By the colours of the images I have of you
In absence crossing streets and making impressions
That I need a hand, like a blind man, and must hide
My thundering heart in tattletale and talk?

Chronicity renders time to spatial images,
Observes components melt and yet still hold
Because of invariances thrust upon the whole;
It tarnishes remembered times, adds weight to hope,
And garners, out of continuity, discreteness.

But my images of you have time there nowhere;
Each is so forced and etched upon my brain
That it sets its own time, crosses out past scales,
And elevates instead new synchrony, time that is now
In soldered terms of times when I can see you.

INNOCENCE #2

Do not give others more than you give to me;
My eyes fail at the disastrous innocence
That writes, "She loves him more; I love her; so,

She can love him." For then I have gone soft,
Like a melted dawn that shudders over snowfalls,
And you will not love me, for you love me harder

The less I soften. So now I pound the sculpture
Of your hair into a massive curl-balled sun
That rises to render my snow-dream red with blood.

THE BROWNS OF WINTER

The browns of winter are melting;
The ochre of grass is effaced with green;
The sky is a lustre of light of incipience;
Radiance goldens the meadows between;

Cardinals cluster the first of the corn strands;
Goldenrods garnish the jonquils and grain;
Remedy now, O ye Dryads of Aestas,
The ice that has frozen the pores of my brain.

THE FORESTS OF MY THOUGHTS

I spread my love and my desire for you like a dreadful mystery
Carpeting the lonely yet still sunlit forests of my thoughts
With spoken flowers, branches, and herbs of finality and truth,
Glades of outspread gladness and perilous hollows of times absent.

For though I can, with quiet analysis and concentration,
Resynthesise each step and sorrow of affectionate lust,
And colour each new problem, or reimage each perfection
With a flaking mind of science carving a cracking porphyry,

A single thought of your hair, a single image of real forestry
Adorned by the movement of you as you sweep aside arraying branches
Or bend to admire a violet, breaks into the arrant woodglade
Of my theories, turns them to wood dust, flattens them to lichen,

And I am transplaced from my desk to a place of imagined mountains
Where I stand and pretend to laugh at the clouds, or cut through the swathes
Of heather in my hastiness to reach you in the singular space
Where you stand, waiting for me, in the forest slopes; round me, birds

Sing, "*Voilà un humain,*" and then my world disappears.
My mind becomes phenomenon, my body a pile of cells,
And one sound pulses, sounding like low and somnolent thunder
Over the vanished world: the beating of my heart in fear.

QUESTIONS, QUESTIONS, QUESTIONS

Do not bewilder me with other men;
I was not born for comparison
But for conquest; but should my heart break,
I can only conquer myself.

Is a man alone? Never;
He is not born for aloneness
But for love; but should his heart break,
He can only love the dead.

Is a woman alone? Never;
She is not born for aloneness,
But for love; but should her heart break,
She can only love her dreams.

Myself, the dead, your dreams—
Was I born for such discrepancies
With life? Make for myself your dreams
To be dead, and then I shall live.

Yourself, the dead, my dreams—
Were you born for such discrepancies
With life? I make for yourself my dreams
To be real; for then you can be

Unbewildered by me and other men.
You were not born for comparison
But for fulfillment; but do you want to be
Fulfilled by a self-conquered me?

CONTROL MODE

I cannot bind the thirsting of my fears;
They break into my poor capacity
For sustenance of sociality;

And when I try to speak of things abstract,
An image of your hands breaks up my dialogue,
And I commence a dark internal catalogue

Of all you are and force myself to stop
And stare at my books until tranquility
Barters my fear for my thought's sterility.

MODERATION

Dream a quiet dream
And then collapse and sleep
Overtones insurgent
Are always there, to keep

Locking of hearts from slumber
And lust from mastery
The flailing of the arrow
Restrains Love's archery

WISHFUL THINKING

Time
Is a scarf
That mantles space into places;

It extends
Like a robe
Across towns and scars and fears;

And it binds
Where you are
To where you were when I loved you;

And it throws,
Like togas
Or mantles from moving statues,

Extensions
To bind you
To where you will be when I find you.

WHERE'ER YOU WALK

I can fear you where you walk
As if your feet raised forests from
The existentially pendant earth.

Internal Matterhorns momentous
Drive me to follow where you walk
To taste of their early winters.

But I do not follow you like a dog;
I try to lead like Orpheus,
Looking back to check on you,

For who will know where you will go
When my back is turned and a gleeful foe
Pleasures you consensually?

INFORMATION

A moment's phone call to someone, when your name came up,
And I was dazzled to commune once more with words.

Did you know that words are analyzable
As information contents, coded for transmission?

My words have so much information they could scream
Under the strain of their improbabilities.

Each is a code of letters quietly scrawled and scribbled,
And every letter signals your persistingness.

NO ANSWER

I tried to reach you, hour on hour, and every minute
Weighed a dark clock of its own. No matter what time it was
When the implausible calls of the ringing flooded your room,
Each emptiness when you did not answer the phone was infinite,
And the silences that answered the bell seemed to loom
Like spectres sitting on a turning wheel, conspiring.

I would invoke the god of Presence for you to answer.
I want the incessant science of your voice to speak
So that the waves of sound be moved to laughter, condensing
Into a box of speech the perfection of your manner
Of saying hello, or the first faint sounds of the tensing
Of your brain to upload grammar into your mode of meaning.

But there was silence. My mind did *not* ask were you were,
But an image of you crossing a street crossed my brain,
And it was lanceted into perspective by upper buildings.
Each time I put the phone down, sometimes annoyed by fear,
Sometimes exasperated, I always felt my heart
Was colouring my images and making me tremble.

LISTENING

I listen to the sounds of women talking
With their tongues spearing the air
As your tongue spears my breath
And leaves cool silence there

EARLY TO RISE

There's always one bird that shouts before them all,
One bird that calls before the dawn begins
And pulls me from my countless daylight dreams
And laughs because I think my virtues sins.

Sing on, sweet bird, and let thy rhythms shriek,
And let thy raucousness riot o'er the roofs;
A million plagiarizings start to shrink
What's beaten forth between thy screeched reproofs.

And whilst thy voice is calling over the town,
Let its dark colloquies of searching shout,
"What is, must be," and "What is not, is not,"
As if *thy* cries were what my life's about.

ART AND ANTIPATHY

Art and antipathy form to yield
Internal and terrible architecture:
The masonry constructed is of grief;
The blocks are stone conglomerates of tears;
Broken the hopes and windows of the walls;
Sculpted and licensed they are of ice.

And yet does not antipathy have fire?
And is not fire constituent of peaks?
And are not flames the congruents of life?
Need ice be all that freezes out of fears?
Is not a single flame enough to form
From floating icebergs caught upon the sea,

Cathedrals that can sing, in burning tones,
New descants to the sun's antiphony?

WHEN EAGLES MEET

When eagles meet,
Will all the broken summers
Hanging on their clawing feet
Fuse to enjoin a firmament
Of spiritless and overturned deceit?

Will their nest die
Like calm and broken branches
Waiting to break without a sigh
And fall in steepest jungle halfway down,
So silently that a bud-burst is a cry?

Or will instead
The clawing form new pinions
Styled and retracted and fed
From interunited blood infused
To a single and unified red?

ARROWS

The blazing archer knows and cries,
With a quivering sheaf of melodies,
That a broken branch from a falling tree
Can be the start of a threnody,
Unless the wound be fought and healed,
And the fallen branch be plied to yield.

CHANGE

No matter what the past was, the future's still the same:
A reckoning and beckoning and follow-through of history;
I could not change, she could not change, we lost.

The silly pomp of tyrants and cold, quiet classic minds
Redecorate my library; Aurelius laughs at me.
I could not change, she could not change, we lost.

I turn the leaves of Poe and see strange faces
Leer at me from gravestones; I drink a glass of wine.
I could not change, she could not change, we lost.

And when the past peers in the form of a new postcard,
I note the postmark silently, coldly interpret the writing.
I could not change, she could not change, we lost.

For if I had changed, we might have met, and my life
Would have been no longer mine and hers no longer hers;
We *could* not change, so lost, nobody's victory.

SUNRISE

Night is dark and warm and womblike,
Flooding oceans filled with pearls;
Through the dim and distant dawnlight
Flock the crows and doves and gulls;

And wide across the eastern shoreline
Trail the wisps of broken stars;
The lights they shed across the wayward
Scarpments are like golden flowers.

And the tarnished mystic's landscape
Fills with a rain of dawnlit light,
Waiting for sunrise to glow and spill
Its viperous basketful of hate.

INEVITABILITY #1

I leave my life no longer to the stars;
No more, frail nether planets, will you hold
Me in metaphoric arms or betray, like the moon,
My light, half crescent or pure full.

And I will, instead, not turn to the flowers—
They are too easy, morning marigolds
And flushing roses, obvious—but to the mind:
I will explore its columns, stalactites,

Obvious analogies to caverns; but when
I emerge, I know the night will spin
Her spinning comets down and drag from me
Hymns to her everlasting Persistingness.

INEVITABILITY #2

I started a poem
On inspiration;
It soon became
Exasperation;

I thought of thought
And what it is:
Moods and moments,
Madnesses;

I thought of you—
But you knew I would!
I was a man
You *understood*!

ENOUGH?

Enough? Oh no, there's lots of verse to come!
Can you not hear the beating of the drum
Like Hector striding strong by Ilium?

No, that was strained, old-fashioned, not quite me;
It was more doggerel that rhymed, a ribaldry.
And yet I sense my mind is breaking free

Again, ready to soar on wings of hope, to make
Appalling lessons out of each mistake,
And, from each paltry argument, to take

Synopses of achievements that reform
The static rhymings raked from every storm
Into new rhymes where fear becomes the norm.

YOUR REVENGE? MY REPLY

My mother and father conceived me,
An easy work of art;
But somehow as an embryo,
I picked up a heart.

I surrounded my heart with a forest
Thick, so the light would not burn;
But you picked, with your clumsiest fingers,
Each leaf, each twig, each fern.

I surrounded my heart then with marble
Carved in an Angelesque stone;
But you made of my marble sheer rockfall
And picked it away like a bone.

So I gently poured beauty around me,
And you, too, to lift us both up;
But you stood on it, smashed it, and broke it
In parts like a pottery cup.

And then my heart was nothing
But blood and muscle and vein;
But somebody else saw its death-throe
And put it together again.

DAMN!

You will not go away, but rise, submerged,
To where the water plays for the pliant moon,
And you spice the rippling waters with desire
While onward the moon climbs up and higher.

You will not go away; you have emerged
From an underworld sea I thought that I had lost,
And now you preen beneath the shining moon
Like a pet who knows it will see its master soon.

The colonnades of our separate selves diverged
In that single moment when I fled your place,
Without a word, headed for booths and bars
And endless efforts to forget my scars.

I stored you away in my poet's idle box;
I got on with life and with inspirers new;
But as I head to where the future lies,
I'm fighting off the pull-in of your eyes.

BRIEF ENCOUNTER

She entered my periphery sidewise, standing
About as tall as me but just behind;
So I was forced to turn, and met an eye
Blinding in its promise of *amour*.
Leftwards I turned the more, to see the smoothened
Youth of her face—and dang! I was suddenly jolted,
For she had the face of my Persistingness,
Though she was younger and more smoothly fleshed.
And Nature zapped in like a stingray, tasering Truth;
So much had Persistingness hurt that I did not dare
To approach this new paragon who tempted me,
This glorious offerer of a match with me,
This loveliness with her natural enticement.

She sensed my shock and fear and hesitation;
Slowly she inched her questioning self away.
Slowly she waited for reciprocation;
Slowly I watched the withdrawal of herself,
And I, because of my past experience,
Knew that no more need Persistingness be my goal.

LaVergne, TN USA
18 December 2010
209250LV00002B/19/P